IMAGES
of America

NORWICH

UNION VILLAGE, VT.

I have now in stock my usual variety of
PHOSPHATES, PLASTER & FERTILIZERS.
I have added a line of

GROCERIES AND HARDWARE.

Which cash secures at living prices.

AGRICULTURAL TOOLS.

Creameries, Churns and Dairy Tools. Sugar arches and Evaporators.

Harnesses! See my stock before you buy. Carriages
and Sleighs. LUMBER.—Shingles, Lath, Flooring, Clapboards and Sheathing. I shall make a specialty of

FLOUR! FLOUR!

Six brands in stock. "Mountain of Snow" beats them all at $6.25. Grass Seed, Seed Corn, Sanford Silo Corn, Meal, Bran and Feed. Cash paid for hides, Pelts, Old Iron, Old Rubber, and all kinds produce taken in Exchange for goods.

No accounts will be run over 30 days. If I buy for *cash* and sell for *cash*, we can both save money.

A. V. TURNER.

A.V. Turner of Union Village regularly advertised his wares in the Norwich town report. According to this 1889 advertisement, Turner stocked everything from sleighs to flour, and traded or paid cash for pelts, old iron, and produce.

IMAGES
of America

NORWICH

Margaret Cheney McNally
and Frances L. Niles

ARCADIA

Published by Arcadia Publishing,
an imprint of Tempus Publishing, Inc.
2 Cumberland Street
Charleston, SC 29401

Printed in Great Britain.

Library of Congress Catalog Card Number: 98-87696

For all general information contact Arcadia Publishing at:
Telephone 843-853-2070
Fax 843-853-0044
E-Mail arcadia@charleston.net

For customer service and orders:
Toll-Free 1-888-313-BOOK

Visit us on the internet at http://www.arcadiaimages.com

This 1820 view of the Congregational Church shows it in its original location on the Norwich Green, facing west, in front of the barracks of Norwich's military academy. The church was moved across the road to its present site on Church Street, facing south, in 1853.

CONTENTS

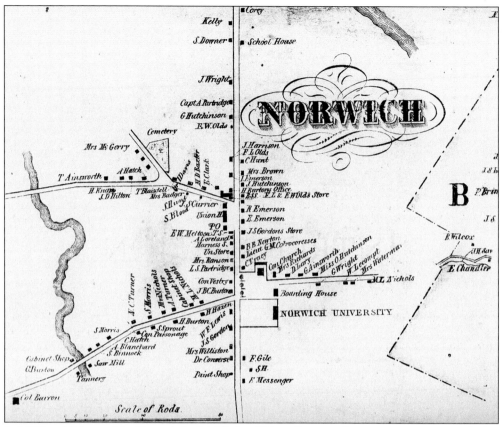

In 1869, publishers of the Beers Atlas highlighted Main Street and major intersections with this detailed illustration in their *Gazetteer of Windsor County*. The map featured numerous residences interspersed with general stores, cabinet shops, a harness shop, paint shop, post office, schoolhouse, hotel, and boardinghouse. Note the prominence of Norwich University, and the industry clustered around Blood Brook on Elm Street—a cabinet shop, tannery, and sawmill.

ACKNOWLEDGMENTS

Special thanks to Kimberly King Zea, whose knowledge of and love for Norwich history were invaluable to the making of this book. Thanks also to the Norwich Historical Society for its documents, maps, and photographs, which make up the majority of the images in this collection; and to Bill Aldrich, Jim Southworth, Elsie Sniffen, Linda Cook, Frank Mefford, Robert Nye, Nicholas and Geraldine Jacobson, and the Norwich Town Clerk's Office, both for their knowledge and for the loan of their treasured photographs. The image on page 38 (top) appears courtesy of the Hood Museum of Art. Photographs on pages 17 (top), 18 (top), 30, 48 (bottom), 51 (bottom), 52, 53 (top), 67 (top), and 107 appear courtesy of Dartmouth College Archives Special Collections.

INTRODUCTION

A photographic history is both limited and liberating. Its limits are set by the history of black-and-white photography, which did not begin until 1839, and by the random nature of what the photographer chooses to immortalize. At the same time, a photographic history can be far more than a record of events—it is liberating for its visual expressiveness, for its ability to capture the immediacy of the moment. This collection, then, is a window on the history of Norwich. Like photography, it begins with the mid-1800s, almost a century after the first European settlers set foot on the banks of the Connecticut River. And as a window, it presents the best visual images of our past, rather than a complete chronicle of town events.

The actual beginnings of Norwich Township date back to early 1761, when surveyors for the governor of the Province of New Hampshire came north up the frozen Connecticut River and marked off, at 6-mile intervals, townships on both sides of the river. Between a hemlock blazed with the number six and an elm marked as number seven stood the area we now know as Norwich, Vermont.

Between the hemlock and the elm, extending 6 miles inland, lay a hilly, thickly forested wilderness—terrain far more rugged than the Connecticut settlers had requested in their bid to settle the uncharted north. They came for a promise: that in return for 100-acre lots, they would agree to cultivate five of every 50 acres of land every five years, preserving all suitable pine trees for masts in His Majesty's Royal Navy.

The first settlers were a homogeneous group, having lived within a short distance of one another in eastern Connecticut. Many were friends of the Reverend Eleazar Wheelock, who would arrive within a few years to establish Dartmouth College across the river in Hanover, New Hampshire. All shared the kind of stamina and determination it would require to subdue the northern wilderness into the farming community they envisioned for themselves and their families.

The pattern for these men was a rugged one: to spend summers clearing land and return to Connecticut in autumn, preparing for the eventual arrival of wives and children. The final journey with family in tow was no small undertaking, through 150 miles of roadless forest on foot or by packhorse. Some preferred to navigate upriver in log canoes, making 8 or 9 miles a day and portaging around falls and rocks. When John Hutchinson made the final trip north in the fall of 1765, he brought only a cow and two horses, which carried his wife, two small children, and their furniture. They simply swam across the river when necessary. Mrs. Nathan Messenger, the only woman in Norwich, was the first to hear the five-month-old Hutchinson baby cry from the river bank as the family neared her log cabin at the site of today's Ledyard Bridge. "It was the sweetest cry I ever heard," she later said.

With the construction of the first sawmill in 1766, the settlers acquired the means to build permanent houses. By 1768, the settlement had the essential gristmill, and farmland was being cleared relatively rapidly—at first, mostly on hills and away from streams and rivers, as the heavily forested flatland that now makes up the village center was still too wet. The census of 1771 reported a Norwich population of 206 people, including 40 families with a total of 92 children. There were 26 unmarried men to eight unmarried women.

Important events followed in quick succession. By 1782, a ferry was established across the Connecticut River. As early as 1785, Norwich acquired its first schoolhouse, on the site of today's Congregational Church—the first public grammar school in Vermont. Within 85 years, Norwich would have 20 such schools.

The height of Norwich's prosperity came between 1820 and 1830, a mere 15 years after the establishment of the first post office here. The 1820s saw the construction of Norwich's most architecturally significant buildings, including the Congregational Church; the impressive brick barracks of the American Literary, Scientific, and Military Academy (later Norwich University); and a number of stately Colonial and Georgian homes. The town center had several stores, a tavern, mills, and mechanics' shops of various kinds. In 1830, the population reached its 19th-century peak of 2,316.

By 1848, when the Connecticut & Passumpsic Railroad completed its line through to the Norwich-Hanover station, the town's population had begun to dwindle. Emigration westward began in the 1840s, and the census of 1850 showed only 1,978 inhabitants. A further decline occurred after the removal of Norwich University to Northfield, Vermont, in 1866, and continued as late as 1900, when Norwich's population numbered only 1,303.

Until the age of the automobile, much of this population was spread out in self-contained communities within the Norwich town limits. One-room schoolhouses doubled as social centers. Each hamlet—Beaver Meadow, Union Village, Pompanoosuc, Lewiston, and Norwich Plain—had its own personality and traditions along with its own church, schools, mills, stores, and post office. Each had its long-standing families, whose names can be seen today on road signs and buildings. These families belied the cliché of the isolated rural community, for they were an eclectic lot—farmers, educators, legislators, lawyers, and jacks-of-all-trades. As this book will show, work was central to their everyday lives, but they found ways to lead full and varied social lives as well.

Other aspects of the past will not show up in this photographic history. The constant threat of disease, for example, is only hinted at—there's the Pattersonville chair that can do double-duty in the sickroom, and the Beaver Meadow stagecoach house situated near a "pest house," reserved for smallpox victims. And no photographs remain of the Town Farm, where paupers lived, though its records appear in town reports from 1844 to 1923.

Ultimately, the Norwich on the pages of this book was determined by the photographers themselves. With the exception of formal portraits, few scenes were the work of professionals—and in some cases a posed portrait, showing the idealized image the subject preferred to project to posterity, was rejected in favor of a lesser-quality scene that better revealed the nature of everyday life. Many, perhaps superior, black-and-white images may still reside in individual collections—and it is to be hoped that this anthology will inspire further gifts to public archives and museum collections such as that of the Norwich Historical Society, which supplied most of the images shown here.

—MCM

One

VILLAGE VIEWS OF MAIN STREET

A well-dressed crowd gathers in front of the first Norwich Inn on Main Street in the 1860s. The stately mansion, built by the wealthy Col. Jasper Murdock in 1797, had two large wings, formal gardens, and a fishpond fed by a log pipe from a spring some distance away. Murdock welcomed stagecoach travelers to his home, which later became an inn and tavern known variously as the Norwich Hotel, Curtis Hotel, and the Union Hotel. Amazingly, the completion of his mansion came only 30 years after Jasper, as a boy of eight, traveled with his family by dugout canoe from Connecticut to the wilderness known as Norwich.

This picture of the Norwich Green in 1860 was taken about eight years after the Congregational Church was moved from its original site facing west on Main Street to its present location, facing south. This was not the first town center; before the Revolutionary War, residents chose the hill visible in the far left of this photograph to be the site of the town's meetinghouse. Constructed in 1785, the meetinghouse was surrounded by a school, store, law office, and several residences. It held its last service on December 28, 1817, and the building's

lumber was sold to Constant Murdock for $100. That same year, residents completed the impressive neoclassical Congregational Church on Norwich Plain. The Revere bell in its steeple is the oldest of six Revere bells remaining in Vermont. Visible to the left of the church in this pre-Civil War scene are the farm buildings and fenced barnyard of the Tracy home, with Norwich cadets shown drilling in the foreground.

The green in 1862 was dominated by the North and South Barracks buildings of Norwich University. The four-story brick structure on the right was built in 1819 to house the American Literary, Scientific, and Military Academy, founded by Norwich resident Capt. Alden Partridge and rechartered in 1834 as Norwich University. When its doors opened in 1820, the Academy offered 42 rooms for one hundred cadets and 5-acre parade grounds with a high fence and two brick guardhouses.

The North Barracks (above) was all that remained after a fire spread from a defective chimney and destroyed the South Barracks in March 1866. More than two hundred people stood helplessly in the snow as a wooden-pail brigade failed to prevent the building from burning to the ground. Onlookers saved books and furniture, but there "were quite a number of guns burned; we could hear them go off." Norwich University was moved to Northfield, Vermont, and the North Barracks became the site of the Norwich Classical & English Boarding School from 1867 to 1877.

The goal of Norwich University was not to lead cadets to adopt a military career, but to give them "a strength of body and manly carriage seldom found amongst merely academic students." Founder Partridge, in stressing the training of the "enlightened citizen-soldier," was considered a maverick in his time. His cadets were famous for their "pedestrian marches," in which groups of 30 to 80 marched as far as Burlington or the White Mountains, often covering 60 miles in a day.

In 1897, fire destroyed the remaining North Barracks building (lower left, opposite page). Public school classes had been held there for ten years, with grammar and high school instruction on the first floor, a family apartment on the second, and a large hall on the third. The official District no. 1 schoolhouse, shown here in 1912 and still in use today, was erected over the ruins of the North Barracks in 1898.

Today's village center was known as Norwich Plain or Burton's Plain. Jacob Burton came to Norwich in 1765 to make plans for the first sawmill. By 1772, he and his sons had cleared more than 60 acres in the center of town. He helped write Vermont's Declaration of Independence and was a member of the state's Constitutional Convention. This pre-1897 picture shows the North Barracks and Congregational Church at far right and the first St. Barnabas Church (center).

In 1902, sleigh was a common mode of winter transportation. This young woman traveled from the Gilman Rogers home on Turnpike Road to Norwich Plain.

Man-about-town Dr. W.S. Bowles was a dentist and proprietor of the inn in the late 19th and early 20th centuries. He and his wife were famous for hosting elaborate social events, and his stylish horse and carriage were frequently seen around the green.

The first St. Barnabas Episcopal Church, shown here, was built in 1863 facing north, next to the military parade ground. It was well supported by then-Norwich University president Edward Bourns and his cadets. The Italianate-style building burned in February 1917, and a structure sympathetic to the original church design was erected in 1918, this time facing west onto Main Street.

The corner of Main and Church Streets presented a different vista before the construction of Tracy Memorial Hall in 1939. Cyrus Tracy, a boot manufacturer, owned a sizable in-town farm on the site, and his carriage barns extended to the Congregational Church. His son, cabinetmaker James Tracy, retired to the family homestead in his old age. Without any heirs, he followed the advice of his friend Dr. L.B. Jones and bequeathed the corner lot and house to the town of Norwich.

Tracy Memorial Hall was dedicated on June 14, 1939. The new town hall also served as a post office from 1940 to 1951. Notice the stately elm tree at the corner, and the newly paved road.

The Norwich Inn, known as the Curtis Hotel from 1800 to 1840, was the first tavern in Vermont to entertain a president. In July 1817, James Monroe addressed the townspeople from the second-floor balcony and then "partook a dinner, prepared in handsome style." This photograph, taken around 1887, shows the home of James Currier on the right and the hotel on the left, then renamed the Union Hotel. On December 18, 1889, a fire started in Edward W. Olds's general store next door and quickly destroyed the store, hotel, and Currier mansion.

With local backing, in large part from Baxter Newton, proprietor W.S. Bowles rebuilt a grand hotel in the Victorian style on the foundation of the burned Union Hotel. The newly christened Newton Inn opened its doors in 1891 and boasted two turrets, "stick style" porches, and decorative shingles in alternating shapes. Annual balls, given by proprietor Bowles starting in 1885, were elaborate affairs with orchestras, promenades, and invitations to "many from Hanover."

The newly rebuilt Newton Inn was connected by a second-story bridge to the general store next door. The large room above the store, known as Union Hall, was the site of town meetings from 1891 to 1939. One resident remembers "elbowing your way through the atmosphere, which was half tobacco smoke—from cigars, mostly—and half the fragrance from the manure on people's boots." Union Hall was the site of many social events, including plays and Grange dances.

Two stores once shared the space now occupied by Dan & Whit's general store. On the left, A.H. Merrill sold dry goods, groceries, hardware, flour, and feed; on the right, E.W. Olds sold clothing and boots and ran the post office. Standing out front in this turn-of-the-century picture are Ada and Arthur Merrill, Edward W. Olds, Sam Morrison (who owned a harness shop at what is now Grange Hall), and Frank Blanchard, mail carrier.

Leon F. Merrill took over Merrill's General Store in 1920, and his wagons offered house-to-house delivery every afternoon. In 1955, Merrill sold the store to Dan Fraser and Whit Hicks, who had worked for him for more than 20 years. Dan, Whit, and their wives staffed the store themselves and decided to attract more business by adding newspapers, beer, wine, and longer evening hours. The Fraser family continues to operate Dan & Whit's—now the town's only general store and a major hub of activity—with the promise, "If we don't have it, you don't need it." Shown here, in 1961, are Whit Hicks, John Fraser, Dan Fraser, meat manager Donny Ballam, and clerk Jessie Stanley.

A corner store stood at the intersection of Main Street and Beaver Meadow Road from the 1790s until after World War II. The original store, operated in the 1800s by the mercantile firm of F.L. & E.W. Olds, burned in 1875. For ten years there remained only a cellar hole overgrown with weeds. The present building, shown here, was built on the site in 1886 and was known variously as Fred Hawley's store, Willey & Smith, Gill's store, and Newcomb's. It now serves as office space.

In the 1930s and 1940s, Gill's store was a popular hangout for Norwich youth. Rob Olds was famous for his generous 5¢ ice cream cones (free if you had just won a Little League game). At the soda fountain, Mrs. Gill served hot chocolate and memorable sundae toppings.

On June 28, 1864, a company of the Vermont State Militia marched down Main Street, in front of the Elihu Emerson home, as part of their "June training." During the Civil War, Norwich furnished 178 men for the Union Army, out of a population of 1,759. They ranged from 15 to 44 years of age. By the end of the war, 27 Norwich men had laid down their lives.

The building at the corner of Carpenter and Main Streets has seen many incarnations, starting with its use as the Union Store in the 1860s. Then-proprietor Joseph K. Egerton was a merchant tailor, town treasurer, and Norwich University trustee. Since then, the building has been the site of Egerton's store, a First National Store in the 1930s, Norwich Electric in the 1940s, Hill's Real Estate & MacDonnell Insurance in 1962, and more recently McLaughry Real Estate and Ledyard Bank.

This 1890 view from the cliff above Norwich shows a village clustered along its Main Street and surrounded by in-town farms and fertile fields. Looking south across the Norwich Plain, one can see the rural character of the land now dominated by Route 5 and Interstate 91. Prominent in the foreground is the Hazen farm, just south of the present Norwich Library.

One of the largest in-town dairy farms was owned by Arthur Leroy Douglass, shown here atop his hay wagon. He married Annie Brigham in 1896 and started a dairy business on Main Street, delivering milk to customers in Hanover, Lewiston, and Norwich for 44 years. Douglass's herd used to walk down Main and Mechanic Streets to their pasture near Blood Brook. Livestock was a common sight on Main Street well into the 1950s.

Arthur Leroy Douglass donned more formal clothes for this portrait in front of his Main Street home in the 1890s. Also in the picture are Mrs. Baxter Newton, the former owner of the elegant home, and Douglass's wife and children. Besides running his in-town dairy farm, Douglass was a member of the University Grange, a school director, and a deacon of the Congregational Church for more than 40 years.

In 1910, cabinetmaker Victor Chester Bushway posed in front of his Main Street brick home with his children, Tom, Stuart, Marie, and Verna. In later years, it was not uncommon to see young Tom and his friends driving cattle from Elm, Church, or Main Street to pasture on Armstrong Hill (now known as Willey Hill).

A picket fence frames a peaceful summer scene in 1910. In front of this Main Street home are owner Lizzie Haskell (center), her daughter Blanche Haskell Taylor (right), and Miss Ellen Hutchinson. Mrs. Haskell was a charter member of the Norwich Women's Club and the Fidelis Bible Class; Blanche taught third grade at the village school.

Minnie Willey Fitzgerald (center) ran a millinery shop in her Victorian house, designed and built by her husband Fred, who was town constable from 1902 to 1950. The house was a popular stopover for the many hobos who followed the railroad tracks up the Connecticut River. Minnie fed them and gave them a night's lodging in the two-stall jail in the barn. Fred, a fastidious man, used to give his pigs a weekly bath with a broom and sudsy water.

Whether by wagon or sleigh, many residents relied on horses to make their way around town. Most village homes had carriage houses and barns, and transportation was an open-air experience. Above, a carriage pulls out of the Douglass yard. Below, Dr. W.S. Bowles and a passenger make their way down a snowy Main Street.

Two

VILLAGE VIEWS:
OUTLYING AREAS

Elias Waterman drives through the covered bridge from Hanover into Lewiston, about 1915. Lewiston, the section of Norwich where Blood Brook meets the Connecticut River, was named after Dr. Joseph Lewis, who came from Old Lyme, Connecticut, in 1767 and settled at first in a log house in the woods south of Blood Brook. He practiced medicine for more than 55 years, making house calls from Thetford to Hartford by horseback or showshoe. He owned a two-story inn on the riverbank and operated a ferry from the natural landing near his home, giving free rides to churchgoers and farmers who brought grain to his gristmill. Over a period of two hundred years, Lewiston, the section of Norwich where Blood Brook meets the Connecticut River, boasted several mills, farms, a creamery, icehouse, coal company, shoe-repair shop, stores, post office, and a busy railroad station. It was a stop for the annual log drives and saw the construction of five bridges between Norwich and Hanover.

Lewiston's "Depot Hill" was a busy community, with three mail trains passing through every morning and three in the afternoon, plus eight passenger trains daily. In one of history's small ironies, the village that thrived as a transportation hub for Norwich was eventually destroyed to make way for a new mode of transportation, the interstate highway, in 1967.

Local people used the trains regularly, whether to commute to job sites such as the Wilder Paper Mill or simply to shop in nearby towns. A typical excursion might involve catching the 6:30 a.m. train in Lewiston, switching in White River Junction, and going on to Lebanon to shop for clothes—perhaps not returning home to Norwich until eight at night.

The railroad was built through Norwich in 1848, and the station was erected in 1884. Over the years, steady streams of Dartmouth students crowded onto stagecoaches to ride from Norwich Depot across the river into Hanover. This picture was taken in 1903, when it cost 25¢ to ride atop the coach.

A crowded platform awaits the 11:20 in Norwich's busy railroad station. The station was closed in 1960.

The Raycrafts ran a grocery store for ten years at the intersection near Ledyard Bridge. Their friendly nature earned them the nicknames Grampa and Grammy Raycraft: "They were always interested to know how people were."

This was the sight that greeted travelers crossing Ledyard Bridge into Lewiston: Raycraft's Groceries, a Shell station, and other businesses. One of the pivotal changes in Norwich's history was the destruction of this thriving community in 1967.

This 1911 postcard shows the downhill drive on Lewiston's Main Street toward the Ledyard Bridge. One of Norwich's several post offices was established in Lewiston in 1898 and remained open until 1954.

An early fender-bender draws a curious crowd near Ledyard Bridge in Lewiston. The Leon Lewis house in the background became Raycraft's Groceries in 1957 and was demolished with the rest of Lewiston in 1967.

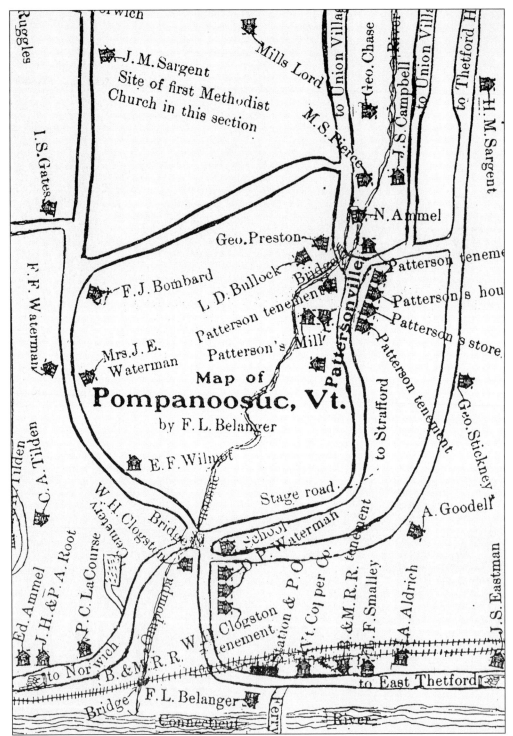

This 1911 map by F.L. Belanger shows the village of Pompanoosuc, the area of Norwich at the mouth of the Ompompanoosuc River also known as Gleason's Flat. Jacob Fenton, Ebenezer Smith, and John Slafter cleared the land for settlement in the summer of 1763.

By 1800, mills churned on the banks of the Ompompanoosuc, producing lumber, lead pipe, grain, and linseed oil. The area boasted its own school, train station, ferry across the Connecticut River, post office, chair factory (above), tannery, and prosperous farms. When the new Wilder dam raised the flood level of the Connecticut in the 1940s, the bustling hamlet was reduced to a few houses.

Leslie "Spencer" Patterson bought a sawmill on the Ompompanoosuc in 1872. He produced lath, lumber, and shingles but soon expanded his line to include chairs, tables, and other furniture. He operated a company store (far left), added a second floor to the factory (back left), and built several duplex tenement houses (three right-hand buildings). The rural context of the factory is seen against the sheep-shorn pasture on the south side of the river, also known as Waterman Hill.

In 1888, Spencer and Julia Atwood Patterson built themselves a home appropriate for an aspiring businessman and his family. The Victorian-style house had fashionable details such as alternating-shaped shingles (no doubt from the factory), wrap-around porch, and polychrome paint scheme. The house was in the hub of Pattersonville, a virtual "company town" within Pompanoosuc. Standing here are Julia Patterson, daughter Lulu Goss, and grandson Harold Goodwin, about 1910.

As a manufacturing section of Norwich, Pompanoosuc attracted factory workers in need of housing. This boy and horse are standing in Pattersonville in front of one of the eight duplex tenements built by Spencer Patterson to house chair-factory workers and their families.

One of two covered bridges crossing the Ompompanoosuc, this span was built in 1866 for $3,990 near today's Route 5. There had been three covered bridges on the same site, built in 1771, 1782, and 1787. At the time this bridge was dismantled in 1954, it was one of only eight Windsor County bridges made with a "town lattice truss"—unique in that its trusses were made of squared timbers instead of planks. D.P. Waterman's house can be seen at the north end of the bridge.

The once-prosperous hamlet of Pompanoosuc included this cape belonging to James Campbell, shown here with his family in the 1890s. The homestead can be found in the upper right corner of the map on page 32, between the two roads leading "to Union Village." A rattan chair manufactured at the local Patterson chair factory is featured in the yard.

At the northern border of Norwich, the Ompompanoosuc flows through the area known as Union Village, a fertile valley that offered excellent mill sites and farmland. First named Hallsville (after miller and tavern owner John Hall), the settlement included mills for felt, lumber, and grain—all swept away by the flood of 1869, along with a dam and bridge. The village church was built in 1836 from bricks made by Seth Ellis of Thetford Hill, at a cost of $1,800.

Union Village got its new name from the U.S. Postal Department when a post office was established there in 1830, on the old stage route between Boston and Montpelier. The schoolhouse in the foreground was jointly financed by Norwich and Thetford; it is said that children from the two towns sat on separate sides of the building.

Union Village was an active community with its own Old Home Day, parade, cornet band, plays, and box socials. French & French, the village grocery, was the town's commercial and social center, where men gathered to transact everyday business or to swap tales of the Klondike gold rush, hunting in the Dakotas, or fighting at Antietam.

James Huntley, the son of an established Main Street family, bought the Union Village store in 1946 after leaving the Army Air Corps. He operated it to full advantage for four years, while the 178-foot Union Village dam was under construction just above the village.

Early records mention "immigration settling strongly toward the west hills" in the direction of the hamlet called Beaver Meadow, or West Norwich. Before 1840, the population of Beaver Meadow equaled, if not exceeded, that in the center of town. At its peak, it supported two churches, a well-stocked store, blacksmith shop, cider mill, sawmill, post office, farms, and a school filled with as many as 60 pupils in the winter term. Paul Sample memorialized the hamlet in this 1939 oil painting.

Often isolated by impassable dirt roads, Beaver Meadow could be a "hard and lonely place" in winter. A solution came in 1915, when retired teacher Margaret Kerr urged residents to build a chapel to serve as both church and community center. Early preachers came from nearby towns and from Dartmouth College. One Dartmouth student remembered, "People were so hospitable that we were dated ahead for dinner sometimes four to five weeks in homes all over the Meadow."

This "old stagecoach house," built in 1779, stands near the intersection of Beaver Meadow and Tucker Hill roads. Tradition maintains that it served as a resting place for travelers on the coach road from Boston to Montpelier. An unusual "pass-through" pantry with Dutch doors on both ends occupies the front hall and may have served as a bar for tavern rooms on either side. Just to the east of this structure, Norwich established a "pest house" in 1797 to house smallpox victims.

The friends in this 1916 scene on the Charles Wallace farm have some well-known Beaver Meadow names. Standing at left are Charles Wallace, Edgar Edmonds, Henry Burnor, and Robert Wallace, with Andy Hodgdon seated in front and Charles Hodgdon riding a young pair of steer.

Long the home of Aaron Edmonds, this house also served as the Beaver Meadow Post Office from 1890 to 1906. Gus Rix ran the stagecoach route between Beaver Meadow and the Norwich Post Office, carrying milk from surrounding farms to the village along with the mail. On difficult spring and winter days, it could take three hours to travel the 5-mile stretch.

Two school friends, Lawrence Wallace and Frances Burnor, stand on a Beaver Meadow hillside. Along with about 12 other pupils, they attended the one-room schoolhouse known as District no. 3. Pupil enrollment peaked at around 60 in the 1790s and early 1800s and dwindled to 11 in the 1940s. The school was closed in 1946, when Beaver Meadow children started attending school in Norwich village.

Among the important roads and byways of Norwich is New Boston Road. Pictured here around 1880 is the farm of David Pratt Sargent, one of the "progressive New Boston farmers." Even the children of New Boston were celebrated in the 1800s for their spirit of "industry and fidelity." When the generous citizens of New Boston rebuilt their schoolhouse in 1905, they made it "one of the best school buildings in town . . . with a sweet-toned bell in the tower, to the music of which the children cheerily respond, and enter more heartily upon their work."

Paul and Fred Metcalf, with their sister Abbie, were the fifth generation of Duttons to work the farm on Dutton Hill, the area settled in the 1700s by their ancestor Samuel Dutton. Shown here in 1939 with their pung sleigh, Paul and Fred were lifelong bachelor farmers. Somehow, Fred found a way to balance his passion for music with the seasonal demands of farming—composing music, giving piano and organ lessons, and playing organ for Sunday services at four area churches.

Out along Union Village Road stood the Gilman family farm. In 1912, William Gilman posed in front of his house with his horse and family: son Lee, wife Mahala Adeline Harvey, son Clyde, and daughter Ruth. Mrs. Gilman, who died in 1960 at the age of 92, attributed her long life and good health to "a lot of hard work and much time spent outdoors."

Bragg Hill Road bears the name of the family who lived in this brick cape built in 1830 at the top of the hill—or, as the deed reads, "the home place of 150 acres more or less known as the 'Cloud Farm,' about two and a half miles westerly of Norwich Village on the road to Sharon." Bought by Francis Bragg from John and Lucinda Cloud in 1856, the land was farmed by three generations of Braggs—yet before the road was formally named in the mid-20th century, the area was still commonly known as Cloud Hill, after the three Cloud family farms there. The inscription on this 1900 picture reads, "Frank Bragg, his oxen, his ma, his hired man, and dog." The house had neither electricity nor plumbing when Nicholas Jacobson bought it in 1938.

The Brigham family name has been associated with the area known as Brigham Hill for more than two hundred years. Paul Brigham, a captain in the Revolutionary War who served as Vermont lieutenant governor between 1796 and 1820, built the first house on the hill in 1788. Today, three former Brigham houses remain, including this one shown in 1890 with Andrew and Abbie Brigham and their children, Annie, Grace, Will, and Paul Andrew.

On Turnpike Road, across from today's Huntley Meadow, Robert and Ruth Fitzgerald sit with their dog on the stone wall in front of an in-town farm. Popular school games for Norwich children had names like King's Land, Drop the Handkerchief, Who's Got the Button, Clap In and Clap Out, and, of course, Tag and Blind Man's Bluff.

At the intersection of Goodrich Four Corners and Town Farm Road stands the Loveland-Hatch house. The A.R. Hatches were a typical farm family. Looking back on daily life, a resident later remembered, "One of the kids' first jobs was to bring in the wood at night. Next was picking up the eggs. By and by you got big enough you could learn to milk the cow. Milk the cows, clean the stables, let them out to water—you sort of grew up with a job."

Out along Turnpike Road, Gilman and Edith Rogers pose proudly with their family and farm animals, including a horse named Rob and beloved dog Jip, around 1900.

An important intersection once known as Huntley Corners, where north Main Street meets Turnpike Road, was distinguished by a stately elm tree reputed to be the largest in Vermont. Here also was the 140-acre Huntley farm, whose house was built in 1777 by Elisha Partridge. Josiah Huntley stands at left, with his wife Emma and sons Jim and Dale, on the stump of the famous elm, which yielded 27 cords of wood when Josiah felled it.

Whatever the road or its condition, spring fever brings out kids with their bikes. On April 2, 1951, the lineup included Raymond Gary, John Lewis, Jack Fraser, Richard Fraser, John Wilder, and George Fraser. Jack and George later became well known as the owners of Dan & Whit's.

Three
RIVERS AND BRIDGES

Since 1796, six bridges have spanned the Connecticut River between Hanover, New Hampshire, and Norwich. This covered bridge, shown from the Hanover side at the turn of the century, was the fourth bridge on the site. Built in 1859 for about $6,000, it was named the Ledyard Free Bridge because it was the first Connecticut River bridge not to charge tolls—a source of constant friction for early inhabitants. Typical tolls before the construction of the free bridge were "foot passengers, 2 cents; horse and rider, 5 cents; sleigh drawn by one beast, 8 cents; coach, 30 cents; each sheep or swine, half a cent." Notice the settlement of Lewiston on the Norwich side of the river.

This panoramic view of the Ledyard Free Bridge shows the destructive springtime erosion that resulted from clear-cutting on the Hanover hillsides, before white pines were replanted there. Lewiston farms and businesses are visible on the Norwich side of the river. For the five years between the burning of the third Ledyard bridge and the construction of this one in 1859, people and livestock crossed the river by ferry, pulled by hand along a rope stretched across the water.

A sleigh leaves the Ledyard Free Bridge on the Hanover side of the river. The sign over the bridge announces the speed limit for vehicles: "No Faster Than a Walk." In the late 1920s, reinforced arches were added to strengthen the bridge for increased automobile and truck traffic, and a covered pedestrian walkway was added to the north side of the bridge. Bridges were subject to constant wear from floodwaters, log jams, and ice. This one lasted 75 years, until 1934.

Construction of the "new" Ledyard Bridge began in the early 1930s, and a one-lane temporary bridge was built on pilings just south of the wooden structure. In those days, many Norwich high schoolers walked to Hanover for classes. When spring ice took out a section of the temporary bridge, a 2-foot-wide suspension link was quickly made to span the gap. It became a daring game to walk across the swaying catwalk, which sagged almost to the water, without using the hand ropes.

The first steel-and-concrete Ledyard Bridge to span the Connecticut at Norwich was constructed as a WPA project in 1935 at a cost of $153,000—compared to about $12 million for its 1998 successor.

Logging was a profitable industry as early as the 1700s. The Connecticut River log drive was an annual institution until 1915, when 65 million feet of wood traveled the 300 miles from northern New Hampshire and Vermont to sawmills in Holyoke, Massachusetts. During those years, it was as hard to imagine a spring without a log drive as it was to think of a winter without snow. The drives began as soon as the ice went out, when logs were rolled into the river over banks 15 to 20 feet high.

Log jams were the bane of the river men, who did their best to avoid sandbars, rocks, and obstacles such as the hated stone pier that held up the wooden Ledyard Bridge at a narrow point in the river. Breaking up log jams was said to be a "manly art," requiring spiked boots and the ability to ride logs in fast, icy water up to 16 hours a day. The work was dangerous, lucrative, and often heroic.

Trademarks of the log drive were double-ended *bateaux*, Native American river men (reputed to be the best in the world), axes and dynamite for breaking up log jams, and raftloads of horses to haul stranded logs back into the river. The horses were usually sold when they reached Holyoke.

As many as two hundred river men accompanied the annual log drive. In *Spiked Boots*, Robert Pike describes them: "Fellers who went down 'all the way,' as we used to say, were somebody. A man who'd gone down all the way on the Connecticut River drive could get a job on any drive in New England and at top wages. It was dangerous work. The women up here who kissed their men good-bye in the spring never knew whether they'd see them alive and whole again."

To prepare for summer days without refrigeration, Norwich residents often harvested ice from the Connecticut River, as well as from smaller ponds and dammed brooks. The trick was to get the block of ice out before it froze back in again, and then to haul it by horse to be packed in sawdust in the barn or ice house.

In this 1907 river scene, a pulley and boom system helps load huge blocks of ice—usually 22 inches square and 12 inches thick—from the frozen river onto a horse-drawn sled. In summer, ice harvesters peddled the heavy cakes house-to-house for use in iceboxes, while keeping some for their own use.

The swift-flowing Connecticut River was an unpredictable force in Norwich before construction of the Wilder dam. The brand-new Ledyard Bridge faced its first challenge in the spring thaw of 1936, when huge chunks of ice dashed into the bridge pilings and onto river banks, flooding roads in Lewiston, knocking over telephone poles, and cracking trees. Even the railroad tracks were inundated as the river swelled, almost reaching the 1927 high-water mark.

The river played a vital role as transportation route for Native Americans and for English colonists in the 1760s, and during the next 75 years most goods were shipped upriver and down by flatboat. Later, roads and railroad tracks were laid to take advantage of the natural river valley, as seen in this early view of "Loveland curve" between Lewiston and Pompanoosuc.

The Ompompanoosuc River, nicknamed "Pompy," meanders southeast through the towns of Strafford, Thetford, and Norwich, where it feeds into the Connecticut. Pompanoosuc, a hamlet of Norwich, was situated at the southern tip and had its own store, depot, post office, creamery, mills, and factory. This view, looking north, shows the buildings comprising the Patterson Chair Company. The steam from the power plant hints at the industry supported by the swift-moving water.

Ferries did a thriving business on the Connecticut River. This rope ferry, shown in the early 1900s, was located where the Ompompanoosuc meets the Connecticut; other ferries operated at Lewiston (near the current site of the Ledyard Bridge) and at the end of Hanover's Rope Ferry Road. Dartmouth College trustees controlled the rights to all three ferry crossings. In 1785, they leased the Pompanoosuc crossing to Isaac Rogers for 999 years for one-fourth of the income.

The Ompompanoosuc River has seen its share of bridges, old and new. The United Construction Company from Albany, New York, built this iron truss bridge in 1908 to replace the covered bridge shown at top on the opposite page. Both stood at Route 132 near Pattersonville.

A Pattersonville tenement house is visible to the left of this covered bridge. The Ompompanoosuc tumbled over the 10-foot milldam just downstream, providing power to Patterson's chair and lumber factory.

A different covered bridge crossed the Ompompanoosuc near today's Route 5. Built in 1866, it lasted 88 years and weathered many hazards, including the 1936 flood that forced water 4 feet above the floorboards. As circuses traveled the river road in summer months, elephants put even greater strain on the wooden timbers. Garey Waterman, shown here in 1940, helped run a large family dairy business near the bridge, which was torn down—despite protests—in 1954.

The greatest disaster in Vermont's history was the flood of 1927, when three days of November rain forced rivers and streams over their banks. Fertile farmland was ruined, buildings destroyed, and roads, bridges, and railroad beds washed away—a hopeless situation, with a long winter in the offing. Most floods occurred in the spring, usually every four or five years in Norwich until construction of the Wilder dam in the 1940s.

Many compared the spring flood of 1936 to the disaster of 1927. The hamlet of Pompanoosuc was almost completely isolated, with roads flooded both north and south. The little schoolhouse was inundated both times.

Four

AT WORK

"Home, church, and work" was the life pattern for many Vermonters. Long winters, for example, meant that the wood box needed filling seven days a week. Above, more than a score of men pose by a communal woodpile, worked up for the Congregational minister about 1864. Most took great pride in their capacity for hard work. As William Loveland wrote when visiting another state, "It takes a Yankee to take the lead in all enterprise. Give me a live Yankee to get through the work, and he will go through it twice while the rest of the odd ends of humanity are getting started."

Austin Huntley mans the trip rope at the Metcalf barn, 1944. Using a block and pulley system, hay was hoisted from a wagon to the barn loft. This was much easier than pitching the hay into the loft by hand. The trip rope acted as a counter balance, directing the load into the haymow. Neighbors helped one another harvest crops, rotating from farm to farm as the season progressed.

Albert Johnson hayed about 300 acres on Maple Hill Farm around 1950. Before bailing machines became common, hay was cut with a scythe, swept in windrows, and then laid "loose" in the wagon and barn. Not simply piled, the hay was carefully layered in an alternating weave that ensured it would not tip or slide.

Pictured above is Paul Metcalf on a wheel harrow pulled by George, Rob, Topsy, and Gypsy on his Dutton Hill farm. Paul and his brother Fred divided the farm work between them, with Fred preferring to take care of the cows, work in the fields, and do house chores, and Paul preferring to drive the horses, manage the machinery, and raise the garden.

Before the era of snowplows, horses and oxen packed snow down by pulling gigantic rollers made of wooden slats, thus creating smooth surfaces for sleighs and other travelers. With one roller operating in Pompanoosuc and another around Norwich village, it took two to three days to do the town's roads. Bert Cloud, Frank King, and Herman Wight are pictured here, about 1921. Town reports show $54 as a typical wage for four days' worth of "rolling roads."

It was hard work rolling roads after a heavy snow. As Fred Metcalf once recalled, "Where the horses couldn't get through, they shoveled till they could." Kerosene was applied to the roller when the snow started sticking, and children sometimes walked inside the roller just for fun. But no matter how deep the snow, children went to school just the same—"any way they could get there." Note the combination of horses and oxen pulling this roller, about 1921.

Bitter cold made winter work a challenge. In February 1868, Otis Coleman wrote in his diary: "Very cold . . . drawed a load of wood . . . froze my fingers. . . . Mercury 38 below zero. Hard traveling." Here, teamster Elliot Philbrook hauls a load of wood.

Paul Metcalf poses with his horse Scoot and a load of logs in front of his Dutton Hill house and barns.

In spring, children often stayed home from school to help gather maple sap to boil down for the year's supply of sugar. Families made and stored syrup, soft sugar, and sugar cakes; there was little need for white sugar in the house. Here, Frederick H. Johnson III takes a break from sugaring in front of a barn on Brigham Hill.

Vernon Fields boils sap off Turnpike Road around 1920. Sugaring off was no easy task: often the sap refused to run, then gushed all over the place; ice melted into the buckets; the sled got stuck in the mud. But sugaring off was a joy, too, partly for "the old earthly tingle of being close to spring."

Albert and William Johnson and "Mr. C" are sawing wood, March 1950. Albert's wife, Louise, kept a detailed account of life on their farm. In early March, she noted, "After breakfast men went with trucks to draw logs from woods—4 loads." A few days later, "Albert split wood and started tractor." Thereafter for many days, "Men split and sawed wood."

At least three blacksmith shops served Norwich village between 1792 and 1940, including this one next to Fairview Cemetery on Beaver Meadow Road (then Mechanic Street). Jerome Forrest looks out the doorway of his shop, which stood for one hundred years before it was torn down in 1914.

Mailman Collins makes his rounds to the Bragg family farm in the early 20th century. One such carrier wrote, "I used my new Model 4990 Chevrolet every day on my mail route over Brigham Hill, Blood Hill, and over by the David Bragg farm, making a great part of my route over many long and steep hills." Before the era of private telephones, people wrote regular letters back and forth, conveying health updates and family news in a well-preserved chronicle of day-to-day life.

Hood & Company owned this busy creamery south of the railroad station in Lewiston, where many local farmers delivered their cream. Some students dropped off their families' cream as they made their way via horse and buggy to the high school across the river. In winter, ice was cut from the river and stored in the structure in the left of this 1925 photograph.

There were many sawmills and gristmills in early Norwich. Before Jacob Burton built the first gristmill at the mouth of Blood Brook in the 1760s, settlers had to carry their grist to Charlestown, New Hampshire, by canoe down the Connecticut or by foot over rough roads. At best, this trip consumed several days. This photograph shows the gristmill and miller's home at Blood Brook Falls around 1880.

"Flour, grain, feed," advertised Thompson's Gristmill in Lewiston in 1929. Other early industries in Norwich included tanneries, brick masonry, painting, blacksmithing, and harness shops, and manufacturers of furniture, lumber, potash, trunks and harnesses, leather military wear, wool hats, boots, and shoes.

Cutting the famous wheel of cheese, Myra Huntley tends store at Newcomb's (formerly Gill's store), at the corner of Main Street and Beaver Meadow Road. It was the mid-1950s, and Campbell's green pea soup cost 15¢.

Patterson's General Store, shown here about 1890, was an integral part of L.S. Patterson's thriving mill and furniture enterprise in Pompanoosuc, where his workers produced clapboards, lath, shingles, chairs, and tables. Finisher Justin Pennock stands on the upper level where, inside, he applied final sanding and varnishes to furniture. Leslie Patterson stands on the bottom step with hands on hips. Spencer Patterson, his father and company founder, stands in the drive.

WE SELL EVERYTHING.

❧ PATTERSON'S ❧

GENERAL STORE.

OUR DEPARTMENTS.

Dry Goods, Notions and Fancy Goods, Clothing and Men's Furnishing Goods, Groceries and Crockery Supplies, China, Crockery, Glassware and Lamps, Jewelry, Silverware and Millinery, Boots, Shoes and Rubber Goods, Hardware, Tinware and Stoves, Drugs, Paints and Oils. Willow and Woodenware, Agricultural Implements, Furniture, Carriages, Seeds and Harness, Oil Cloths and Wall Paper, Guns, Revolvers and Ammunition, Tobacco, Cigars and Pipes, Five and Ten Cent Goods, Confectionery, Toys, and everything sold in a General Country Store.

POMPANOOSUC, VT.

General stores usually wrapped customers' goods in a package tied with string. Notice the list of goods offered for sale on this 1905 wrapping paper.

When Leslie "Spencer" Patterson purchased a Pompanoosuc sawmill in 1872, he envisioned a mill and furniture company of proportions Norwich had never seen. By 1900 he was shipping products all over the Northeast via the nearby railroad, and the company had grown to include

this two-story factory, where chair parts can be seen suspended in the windows. Three generations of Pattersons are represented here among the factory workers: David, founder Spencer, and his son Leslie.

No. 500, Cabinet.

In 1900 the L.S. Patterson Illustrated Catalog featured 26 chairs, from simple dining seats to elaborate rattan chairs with patented rocking devices. Patterson advertised, "We manufacture right from the log, and as our plant is run entirely by water power we are enabled to quote you the very lowest of prices for first-class work. Our No. 500 Cabinet Chair is doubly useful, as it can be used in any room in the house as a handsome Sitting Chair, when not needed in the sickroom."

Two workers pose with company-produced chairs in the engine room of Patterson's Mill. A kerosene lamp in the background dates the photograph to before 1909, when an estimate was secured for installing electric lights.

Five

AT SCHOOL

In 1785, citizens petitioned the town to form the first school district. By 1869 there were 20 such districts; today there is one. In Norwich, the condition of schools varied widely. Some were "sufficiently commodious, pleasant, and in good repair," while others were very poorly furnished—lacking even a wall map, dictionary, or decent ventilation. The town philosophy in 1877 was that "the school should be more than a place for obtaining book knowledge. It should give training in morals, in manners, in the virtues of everyday life, such as promptness, obedience, and generosity." The District no. 9 schoolhouse, shown here in the early 1900s, was located at the intersection of New Boston and Norford Lake roads. Its 21 students were praised in 1865 for displaying "the best of order, and *no whispering!*"

Scholars from District no. 1 pose in their finest clothes around 1900. They were among the first to attend the new two-story brick schoolhouse built on the town green in 1898, which is still in use today. It then featured four rooms, two grades to a room, for in-town children in first through eighth grades. Before the erection of this building, District no. 1 children attended

school in several successive locations. These included a red schoolhouse (the first public grammar school in Vermont) on the present site of the Congregational Church and, later, the former North Barracks building of Norwich University, a brick schoolhouse at the southern end of Main Street, and even the church vestry.

District no. 1 pupils attended class in the former North Barracks building of Norwich University between 1888 and 1897. At midday, they would climb the rickety stairs to the bell tower to eat their lunch. Children had to keep the fire going in each schoolroom, feeding the long stoves with wood the length of railroad ties.

Norwich Classical and English

BOARDING-SCHOOL,

Scholarship and deportment of

Byron H. Hutchinson

For the Term ending *Nov. 24th* 1879

Arithmetic,	"	Natural Philosophy,	6.5
English Grammar,		Chemistry,	
Geography,		Rhetorical Exercises,	
Spelling,	5.5	Latin,	
Algebra,	6.4	Greek,	
Geometry,		French,	
History,			

Average Scholarship, ... 6.3

Deportment, ... 10

In Scholarship, 10 signifies *perfect* ; 9, *very good* ; 8, *good* ; 5, *indifferent* ; 0, *failure.*
In Deportment, 10, marks unexceptionable conduct.

ERVING L. RICHARDSON,
Principal.

Schools issued report cards measuring both "scholarship" and "deportment." One district's goal in 1879 was, "Morals are not forgotten, but all swearing, quarreling, and insolence to passersby are held in check. In short, a good school is where the teacher secures good order without extreme severity, inspires the scholars to a love of study, sets a good example before them both in school and out, and induces them to imitate it."

Of the 18 Hanover High School students who visited Mount Vernon in 1911, seven came from Norwich. Starting in 1897, Norwich students attended high school in Hanover, often walking both ways across the Ledyard Bridge. The town paid their tuition.

A 1923 group poses in front of "Norwich Public School," the District no. 1 schoolhouse on the green. The brick building was constructed in 1898 at a cost of $5,134 and accommodated all District no. 1 students through eighth grade. At the time this picture was taken, the superintendent of schools had just recommended "that a raise of $1 per week would keep good teachers here." Familiar names in the photograph include Huntley, Sargent, Bradley, Aldrich, and Fraser.

A younger group assembles on the Norwich Public School steps around 1930. Familiar names include Cook, Armstrong, Sargent, Hazen, Parker, Olds, and Ladd.

The 1941 graduating eighth grade, arrayed proudly on the steps of Tracy Hall, included 15 students from in-town, and three each from Beaver Meadow, New Boston, and Pompanoosuc. The last eighth-grade graduation in Norwich took place in 1964, when seventh and eighth graders started attending middle school in Hanover. The grade school was renamed the Marion W. Cross School in 1973, in honor of the longtime teacher and principal standing at far right in the back row.

With teachers arrayed in the back row, the Hanover High School class of 1921 poses for a graduation picture. Following a senior ball at the high school, the class of 20 Norwich and Hanover students attended graduation exercises in a Dartmouth hall. Forty-two years later, in 1963, Norwich and Hanover formally merged their middle and high school systems in the nation's only interstate school district.

The Bicknell School, built in 1827 by the residents of District no. 15 on Bradley Hill, cost $92 plus $8 for a stove, and measured 16 square feet. By 1865, the superintendent lamented that the house was "unfit for such a purpose." He described a January session with students and teacher "huddled and shivering around a stove in the little open shed. But all were disposed to make the best of the situation—a bright and promising set of pupils, a credit to the District."

The District no. 11 schoolhouse served children living halfway out Turnpike Road. As in other schools, there was a high turnover of teachers, who were hired for eight-week terms. One Turnpike teacher resorted to using her riding whip to cure the older boys of their mid-afternoon prank of jumping through a schoolroom window, singing and shouting, and climbing back in the same way. In 1899, the small group of scholars were "some of the most advanced in the rural schools."

Teacher Eva McDonald (top left) looks as young as some of the pupils in her District no. 11 schoolhouse in 1905. The entire school budget that year was $242, including $18 for "wood and kindling" and $210 for Miss McDonald's 30 weeks of teaching. All Norwich families provided their own textbooks—often in the form of hand-me-downs—and even in 1905, nearly half the schools had no dictionaries or any kind of reference works.

In 1907, the District no. 7 children in Pompanoosuc had a lot to be proud of: three years before, the schoolhouse had been in a "state of dilapidation," with supplies so low that each child "was obliged to find their own or go without," and the three dictionaries in town "so far out of date as to be useless." By the close of the year, the schoolhouse was "in as good condition as any in the state, our books are all modern, we have maps, globes, and dictionaries of the very best."

District no. 17's Sproat School, located near the intersection of Turnpike and New Boston roads, had 11 pupils in 1914. Teacher Blanche Haskell poses here with: (front row) Phyla Hazen, Kenneth Stevens, Frank Somerville, Flossie Huntley, and Lawrence Huntley; (back row) Leroy Aldrich, Elwin Aldrich, Alice Bushnell, Maurice Aldrich, and Roy Hazen.

Teacher Mabel Emerson had 13 pupils in her District no. 11 Turnpike school when this picture was taken in 1915. The superintendent that year argued against extending the number of weeks of compulsory school attendance in rural schools: "The condition of highways makes it injudicious for children to go any distance through a large part of March and April. On many Vermont farms also the child is offered advantages in vocational education that the city child does not have."

District no. 3 was established in Beaver Meadow in 1791, and large families filled the school with up to 60 pupils in the winter terms. Conditions in a school like this, which burned in 1921, could be harsh, one superintendent lamented in 1887—with "windows and doors more or less broken. The seats are the old-style board seat, with a cold, frosty wall to support the back, and desks awkward in form and often so marred by the knife of mechanically inclined boys as to be nearly useless."

A new Beaver Meadow schoolhouse opened in 1922 with 15 pupils such as these. For 16 years, they were taught by community mainstay Stella Sears, who would come to school every winter Sunday to start the wood stove and "take the chill off Monday mornings." In the 1940s, enrollment dwindled to 11, and in 1946 District no. 3 was consolidated with the village school.

Norwich University was considered unusual for its liberal, nonsectarian approach to military education, but the cadets' regulation dress and demeanor infuriated their Dartmouth counterparts across the river, "somewhat as a mad bull is said to be affected by a red flag." Between 1836 and the Civil War, feuds were common between cadets and "Darties," with "the banks of the placid Connecticut the scene of many encounters. The possession of the covered bridge was especially contended for." Cadets traveled to Hanover only in groups, risking insults from the Darties ranging from kicks to button snatching. In one skirmish, "the enemy, from roofs and upper floors in Hanover, pelted us with eggs. Many of our force had their coats ripped up the back to the collar." Everything changed as war loomed in 1861 and large numbers of cadets left for the front to be drill masters for New England volunteers. Dartmouth students began to realize that the "military institution in Norwich stood for more than a show of brass buttons, and that the time might not be too far distant when they would be glad to serve under a Norwich man."

In 1867, the Norwich Classical & English Boarding School filled the void left by Norwich University's departure for Northfield, Vermont, by tutoring boys and girls in the old North Barracks. Girls were day students. Twenty boys boarded with the principal's family, receiving "such attention as their ages and circumstances require," while other boys "boarded around." The private school was short-lived, however, and closed in 1877.

During its brief ten years, the Norwich Classical & English Boarding School "fitted several young men for college, and others of both sexes prepared themselves for teaching and active life." For the boarding tuition of $275, they learned Latin, Greek, geometry, algebra, "English Analysis," science, rhetoric, and moral and natural philosophy. Music instruction was available for an extra $12, and students gave orations and musical programs at the Congregational Church.

Boys'
Classical and English
Boarding-School.

REV. MR. AND MRS. WM. H. GILBERT, PRINCIPALS.

ASSISTED BY

A. Eugene Nolen, A. B., of Woonsocket, R. I.

Miss Celia Sherman, of Ansonia, Conn.

Charles F. Emerson, of Dartmouth College.

THE want of a CLASSICAL SCHOOL of high order to fit boys for college and for business, and to furnish a safe, Christian home for those who would come from city and town, to secure its protection and enjoy its literary advantages, has long been felt in Vermont.

A few citizens of Norwich have generously furnished the means to supply this want.

A CAPACIOUS BUILDING,

Every way adapted to the purpose, with ample grounds, has been provided. It contains a Boarding Department, convenient for the family of the Principal and about Twenty-five Boarding Pupils, a large and well-appointed School Room, and a spacious Gymnasium, furnished for the light gymnastics.

The Lodging Rooms are inviting and comfortably furnished, well warmed and ventilated. There is a Bathing Room supplied with hot and cold water.

THE PLAY GROUNDS

Are large and attractive, affording the best facilities for sports in the open air, and, with the Gymnasium, ample means for physical culture.

THE LOCATION,

In the village of Norwich, is, on every account, desirable. It is half a mile from Norwich and Hanover Station on the Passumpsic Railroad. Norwich is pleasantly situated on the Connecticut River, four miles from White River Junction and about one mile from Dartmouth College. It has delightful surroundings, is retired, and free from business excitement and the means of dissipation.

Although it is designed to make

CLASSICAL INSTRUCTION

A speciality in this institution, yet superior facilities will be afforded for pursuing the common and higher English branches, also Modern Languages, Music and Drawing. No pains or expense have been spared to secure teachers highly qualified for their positions.

Six
CLUBS AND OUTINGS

High school seniors dress as angels, kings, and shepherds to reenact the Christmas story every year in Norwich village, with Joseph leading Mary on a donkey to a Main Street barn. Townspeople fill the road as they sing carols and follow Mary and Joseph to the manger scene. This ongoing event is a reminder of the many pageants, plays, concerts, and spontaneous socials that flourished in Norwich before the days of electronic entertainment.

Starting in the 1880s, Union Hall became the site of many dramatic performances, dances, and other social events. Typical admission for a promenade concert was "Gents, 50 cts.; Ladies, free." Plays and musicals were popular forms of entertainment, with townspeople donning costumes and exotic roles. Familiar faces show up again and again in many cast photographs: Emma Slack Huntley, Minnie Davis, Ada Bowles, and Helen Hawley are among the thespians pictured here.

Norwich was the site of so many plays and musicals that it organized its own Dramatic Club. Cast lists were filled with prominent family names. This eclectic 1914 group includes such well-known surnames as Huntley, Cossingham, Olds, Bowles, Bragg, Hutchinson, Bushway, Fitzgerald, Sargent, and Rogers.

The Female Abolitionist Society sponsored this quilting bee in the summer of 1918, with 18 Norwich women showing off their friendship and handiwork.

Christian social clubs were common in the early 20th century. The Congregational Church hosted two large Bible groups, the Fidelis Bible Class and the Mizpah Bible Class. Pictured here is the Mizpah group in 1919; the church hosted the annual convention of the Mizpah Christian Endeavor Union in 1921.

Years ago, village bands were scattered over the countryside. In 1872, a blacksmith named M.S. Colburn (back row, second from left) organized Colburn's Cornet Band of Union Village. In 1877 they were uniformed for about $45 each, and for the next seven years played "more or less well, but always with contagious enthusiasm" everything from marches to polkas at political rallies, picnics, Dartmouth sports events, and the Tunbridge World's Fair.

In 1915, members of the Norwich chapter of the Young Men's Christian Association organized the first and only YMCA band in Vermont. With $1.50 in their treasury, they had to provide their own instruments and instruction books. The band stopped playing in 1942, as members came from a radius of 20 miles and gas rationing made it difficult for them to attend rehearsals and engagements. Their bandstand, built on the Norwich Green in 1915, remains today.

Every September from 1886 to 1894, the Ompompanoosuc Agricultural Fair Society hosted a three-day gala featuring livestock events, horse races, a ladies' driving exhibition, bicycle race, and band music. Special trains dropped off passengers at the fairgrounds and picked them up again at 5 p.m. The annual fair was plagued by rain, and because the bulk of the work fell too heavily on a "few faithful workers," the event was canceled after its eighth year.

Pompanoosuc Agri'l Society.

8th Annual

FAIR

AT

POMPANOOSUC, VT.,

Sept. 12, 13, 14.

PROGRAMME:

FIRST DAY. Tuesday, Sept. 12th.

This day will be devoted to exhibitors for entries and getting stock and articles in proper places for exhibition, and all such entries must be made that day at the Secretary's office, between 9 a. m and 3 p. m. Also all entries for races must be made to the Secretary on or before Sept. 12, 1893, 12 m.

SECOND DAY. Wednesday, Sept. 13th.

9.00 a. m. Filling of Committees at Secretary's office. Also grand exhibition on track of Horses and Stock   Exhibition of Stallions on track for Premiums. Exhibition of Brood Mares and Suckers in rear of Judges' stand for Premiums.

9.30 a. m. Exhibition of Matched Horses on track for Premiums.

10.30 a. m. Drawing Match. Waterman Stakes for Oxen. $10, divided in four parts. 5 per cent entry. Drawing Match for horses. Henry Foster Stakes, $10, divided in four parts, 5 per cent entry.

11.00 a. m. Newton Inn Stakes   For Foals of 1891, trot or pace. $5 with $10 added by Society. Entries payable in two installments, Sept. 1, $2.50, balance Sept. 12th. Half-mile heats, best two in three in harness ; 3 or more to start. Divided 50, 25, 15 and 10 per cent.

11.30 a. m. Ladies' Driving Exhibition. Premium $10, to wagon. 1 mile exhibition required, per order judges. Style of turnout and reins-woman-ship to be considered. Horses entered in races, except Quimby Farmers Race, barred. Contestants required to hold Membership Tickets. Four or more to start, Divided 50, 25, 15 and 10 per cent.

2.00 p. m. Pompa Four-year-old Purse Race. $25, trot or pace, for colts that have never beaten 3 minutes, 3 or more to start, mile heats, best three in five in harness. Entry 5 per cent with 5 per cent from winners ; divided 50, 25, 15 snd 10 per cent.

2.30 p. m. Quimby Farmers Race. $25, open to all horses or mares that have never beaten 3.15. Owners to prove identification if required. This race is for young horses ; ringers barred. Entries and moneys same as previous race.

3.30 p. m. 2 50 Class, trot or pace. $35, 3 or more to start, best 3 in 5 in harness Entries and moneys same as previous race.

THIRD DAY. Thursday, Sept. 14th.

11.00 a. m. Wheelock Stakes for Foals of 1890, trot or pace. $6 with $12 added by Society. Mile heats, best two in three in harness, 3 or more to start. Divided as in previous race. Contestants required to hold Membership Tickets.

1.00 p. m. Bicycle Race. $10. Divided $5, $3, $2. Entrance 5 per cent.

2.00 p. m. Stallion Race. $25. Open to all stallions, mile heats, best three in five in harness, 3 or more to start. Entries and moneys same as Pompa Purse.

2.30 p. m. 3 minute class. $25. For horses that have never beaten 3 minutes to trot, 4 or more to start, best 3 in 5 in harness. Entries and moneys same as previous race.

3.30 p. m. Free for All. $75. 5 entries required, 3 or more to start, trot or pace, best 3 in 5 in harness. Entries and moneys same as previous race.

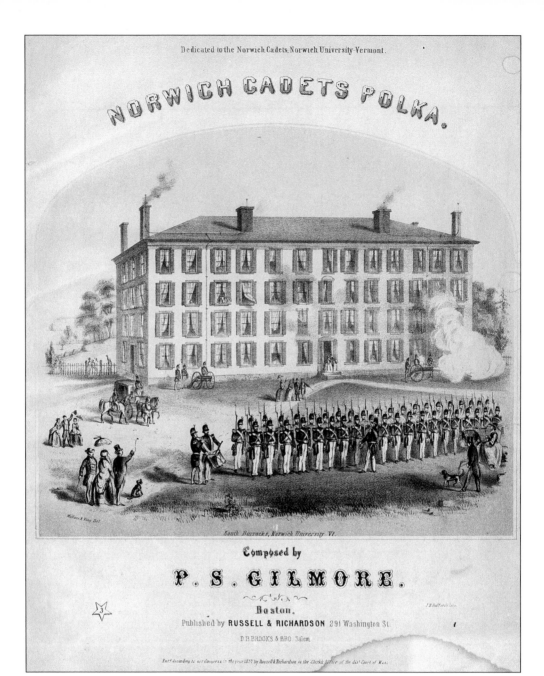

Dedicated to the Norwich Cadets, Norwich University-Vermont.

NORWICH CADETS POLKA.

South Barracks, Norwich University VI.

Composed by

P. S. GILMORE.

Boston.

Published by RUSSELL & RICHARDSON 291 Washington St.

D.B.BROOKS & BRO. Salem.

Ent'd according to act Congress in the year 1857 by Russell & Richardson in the Clerks Office of the dist Court of Mass.

A Grand Celebration!

—— AT ——

"THE MAPLES," - - - - - NORWICH, Vt.

—— ON THE ——

THE GLORIOUS FOURTH!

FIRE CRACKERS & TORPEDOES!!

From Sun-rise till Sun-set!

GRAND BALLOON ASCENSION AT SUN-SET!

BRILLIANT ILLUMINATION AT 8 O'CLOCK P. M.,

—— BY ——

CHINESE AND JAPANESE LANTERNS!

AT 8.30 P. M.

THERE WILL BE

A MAGNIFICENT

DISPLAY OF FIRE-WORKS

—— CONSISTING OF ——

Colored Fires, Bengola Lights, Roman Candles,
Vertical Wheels, Triangles, Rosettes, China Flyers,
Mines, Floral Shells, Young Etnas, Flower Pots, Batteries,
Flying Pigeons and Sky-Rockets!

☞ If the weather should be unfavorable, the above Display will be postponed till the first pleasant Evening.

OUR OWN PRESS.

Today's Norwich Fair began in July 1949 as a three-day event on the green, featuring round and square dancing on Friday night and a parade on Saturday morning, headed by the Grant & Nichols Fife and Drum Corps. There were floats, exhibits by the University Grange, riding clubs, the latest automobiles, and decorated bicycles. Saturday afternoon brought exhibitions of 12 pairs of the finest oxen, gaited horses, lassoing, and cooking contests.

In the 1950s, the Norwich Fair was much the same, with riding clubs and floats following the same route down Main Street to the Norwich Green.

As evening fell, the Norwich Green remained a carnival of lights and music, as fairgoers chased steeple-high thrills on midway rides. On Sunday, little remained to recall the three-day extravaganza. Today's fair continues the tradition, with the fairgrounds removed to Route 5.

Comrey and Mattie Cook won second prize at the first Norwich Fair parade in 1949, driving their 1902 Cadillac. They were parading in the same car when this picture was taken around 1970—and even in 1997, Comrey rode in the town parade at age 103.

Oxen competitions have featured prominently in each year's fair. These are two of the many successors to the famous string of oxen entered by Glen Parker and Arthur Maxwell in the driving and pulling contests at the first Norwich Fair.

"Old Home Week" in Vermont.

PRES. H. V. PARTRIDGE.
1ST VICE PRES., T. A. HAZEN.
2ND VICE PRES., G. M. SLACK.

SEC., F. W. HAWLEY.
TREAS., GEO. MESSENGER.

August 10 to 16, 1902.

"How dear to my Heart are the Scenes of my Childhood."

The Norwich Old Home Association most cordially invite you to return and participate in the

Second Annual Reunion

of present and former residents,

Old Home Week,

August 10 to 15, 1902, and especially

to be present at the

Public Exercises, Old Home Day,

Norwich, Vermont,

Friday. August 15, 1902.

Please signify to the Secretary your acceptance of this invitation at your earliest convenience.   Respectfully.

MISS S. J. BURTON,   MRS. ELLEN LOVELAND MATTHEWS,
MISS CARRIE GODDARD.   Committee on Invitation.

In 1901, citizens organized the Norwich Old Home Week Association to "promote the welfare of the town by increasing the interest in the town among former residents." Invitations like this were mailed to 388 former Norwich residents in Vermont and other states. About one thousand people showed up on the green for dinner, an open-air concert, and speeches. Buildings were illuminated for the occasion, and windows everywhere were ablaze with light.

Sunday was always "go to Meeting day," an occasion for dressing up and taking the air on the way to church. Mrs. Dale Bullock donned fur to ride in this sleigh near the Pattersonville factory settlement around 1900.

This 1910 photograph is inscribed on the back: "Cousin Fenno & his son, Joe Dewey, took us Colemans for a ride when Joe graduated from Dartmouth College." Cousin Fenno left the driver's seat to take the snapshot of Celia, Margaret, and Louise in the back seat, and Zenas Coleman in the front.

The Colemans and Johnsons take their hay wagon on a Sunday picnic, about 1930. Sunday afternoons were reserved for rest and recreation, neighborly visits, and midday family dinners. In the summer, these rituals sometimes found expression in hilltop excursions. The Colemans enjoyed picnics on top of Armstrong Hill, which offered a commanding view down the Connecticut River Valley.

Ruby Fitzgerald and the "telephone girls" take a spin in an automobile in the early days of electronic communication. Ruby's family ran the town's first telephone system out of their home on Main Street, providing service from 7 a.m. to 9 p.m. on 29 party lines for about 70 customers. Ruby began her telephone career at age 15 at the switchboard in her parents' home, ending up 48 years later as chief operator for New England Telephone & Telegraph in White River Junction.

Croquet, anyone? Rev. Nathan R. Nichols, minister at the Congregational Church for 27 years, poses at his Elm Street parsonage with his wife and family. The popular minister, who began his career in Norwich in 1880, was known for his "quiet gleam of humor" and "charity towards all."

Caroline Fowler Hazen, who lived from 1842 to 1918, is dressed for an "Old-Fashioned Concert," a popular form of entertainment in her youth.

Anna Converse joins a ladies' shooting party on the west side of Main Street, looking south. Miss Converse lived in the first of the three brick houses at the entrance to Norwich. She was a mainstay of St. Barnabas Episcopal Church, serving as organist, sacristan, and treasurer from the 1890s until her death in 1917. Her sisters, in Anna's memory, gave the parsonage next to the church.

While live music was a popular pastime at Union Hall, entertainment could be found at home as well. On an evening in Beaver Meadow, Hattie Edmonds and her mother relax to the scratchy tones of a hand-wound phonograph.

The Norwich Pool, shown here around 1945, was created by damming up the Charles Brown Brook—one of the first accomplishments of the newly formed Norwich Development Association. For many years, Norwich schoolchildren gathered at the pool for a year-end celebration and picnic.

"Norwich Skiway," shown here in the 1960s, featured a rope tow above Elm Street near Hillside Cemetery. Norwich had one ski jump and at least two other ski hills with their own rope tows. Sledding was another winter essential. The typical traverse sled could seat six, and in the days before plowed roads and salt, children could travel at a "pretty good clip on almost glare ice," sailing through the village from Willey Hill, past St. Barnabas Church, down the hill on the road to Wilder.

Seven

EVERYDAY LIFE

It was a good life, after the day's work was finally done. Relaxing with their pipes are Charles Ensworth, Charles Loveland, and Aaron Loveland. All three were grandsons of Joseph Loveland, one of the original settlers from Connecticut. The two Loveland brothers came from a family of 13 children. Aaron was a member of the state legislature in 1888. His brother Charles, who drove the town hearse, was reputed to be "one of the gruffest men one could meet."

Anna Converse writes at her parlor desk around 1900. Her large house on Main Street was one of several elegant brick homes owned by the Converse family in Norwich. Built between 1810 and 1830, these houses featured warm, soft brick made in a brickyard on Blood Brook near Christian Street.

Hattie Dutton Metcalf holds her infant daughter, Abbie, in 1903. Abbie and her brothers, Paul and Fred, lived on their Dutton Hill farm all their lives. Abbie would later write, "Up here we still have trilliums blooming in the woods and deer. At night I can look up and see Orion, Pollux, and Castor and all the others. I don't need pipes full of water to freeze, or central heating I can't afford. I like it the way it was when Mother and Father were here, and my brothers."

Minnie Willey Fitzgerald (left) gathers summer bouquets with a friend. Minnie, born in Norwich in 1876, ran a millinery business from her Main Street home. She visited Boston twice a year to keep up with the latest styles, and decorated her hats with feathers, ostrich plumes, little bunches of fruit, and veils.

Frank Bragg, a farmer and excellent hunter, kept his gun rack on the kitchen wall in his brick farmhouse. A room like this would make a warm refuge during the worst winter days—but even so, as one Norwich diary entry recorded, "It was not uncommon to warm feet by a fire while hands in the lap froze." In the early 18th and 19th centuries, blankets were often hung from iron hooks in the ceiling to trap warm air in a localized niche.

Two dogs face a winter day on the Bragg home place. A Norwich diary entry in February 1898 described a typical day following a storm: "Snow. Snow. Snow. It snowed all last night and the wind blew quite hard. Snow is drifted. Father had to make a path to the barn. We have done the work and boiled victuals for dinner and baked an Indian pudding. Mother mended. Mr. B. broke out the road and Dana came up with his steers. In some places it was the worst storm in years."

Dorrance E. Sargent relaxes with a cat in his barn on Main Street. Born in 1882, Sargent was variously a farmer, horse and cattle dealer, owner of a general store, selectman, and chef. He earned some fame as a weather prophet. In December 1932 he predicted a cold winter: "Although bears have not denned up yet and there has been no snow for deer to yard up, animals are heavily coated, which indicates that we will have plenty of cold days in February."

Mina Cutting married Dorrance E. Sargent in the Congregational Church at the turn of the century; they celebrated their 61st anniversary in 1963. There was, of course, the never-ending cycle of kitchen chores, but she also belonged to the University Grange and Norwich Women's Fellowship and helped Dorrance run the corner store known as Gill's in the 1930s.

Returning from chores is Eunice Wallace; she married Charles Wallace in 1895, had two sons, and lived on a farm in Beaver Meadow. Anticipating the demands of winter, people seldom took time to drive to town in summer; they needed every moment to prepare for the long, cold siege.

Mrs. Parkhurst hangs her winter washing in 1935. Many Norwich families made their own soft soap, using wood ashes and fat. After the clothes were scrubbed on a board and boiled, a cup of this homemade soap was added.

It is pickling time in Eunice Wallace's Beaver Meadow kitchen. Mrs. Wallace was also known for her wild strawberry preserves, raised doughnuts, and apple pies. In summer she concocted "switchel," a ginger-based drink for hot days in the hay field that "might bite your tongue a little bit."

Lefavor B. Jones, "horse and buggy doctor of Norwich," poses with his horse Bradley on the green. Born in 1877, Dr. Jones was the town's health officer and beloved physician for 37 years and was reputed never to have lost a patient to pneumonia. Three generations could attest to his skill and philanthropy: "He hurried to bedsides to relieve the suffering of patients and the anxiety of parents—under road and weather conditions that would preclude the going out by many."

Andrew Thorburn, Frank Somerville, Harlon Richardson, and Vernon Field pose together. In 1919, the superintendent cited Andy and Vernon for attending Turnpike School for a year without an absent mark. Frank grew up to run his family's dairy farm on Turnpike Road, while Andy followed Vermont's "jack-of-all-trades" tradition—driving school buses, plowing roads, and offering moonlight sleigh rides to Dartmouth students along Norwich's back roads.

In a patriotic effort to spot German planes during WW II, Norwich residents built several watchtowers. The two-story watchtower shown here was located on Meetinghouse Hill, just off Union Village Road. Chief observer Comrey Cook scheduled volunteers in three-hour shifts, night and day, seven days a week. One observer, Fred Metcalf, used to read H.G. Wells and Shakespeare or compose music while on watch.

This informal group of schoolmates, gathering for a picture on the green around 1920, includes Joseph Merrill, Ned Cossingham, Thayer Lewis, Gail Barrett, and Evelyn Goodrich.

The Norwich Public Library was dedicated in 1902. At first, books were kept in the Congregational Church vestry, and later in the barracks of Norwich University. Forty public-spirited citizens contributed so generously to the building fund that they raised $2,414 by 1902—a notable achievement for a small community at the turn of the century. Mary (Mrs. Edward) Olds was the first librarian in 1880, and through the years various members of the Olds family were active in the library.

Members of the all-volunteer Norwich Fire Company, formed in 1920, line up in front of Tracy Hall in 1939. Behind them on the right is the company's pride and joy, a 1938 Ford pumper capable of spraying five hundred gallons of water per minute. To the left is their first gas-powered fire truck, a 1928 Chevrolet. Before 1920, a chemical tank on a horse-drawn wagon was the only formal means of fighting fires. In the center, in front of the door to Tracy Hall, is Chief Harold Kingsbury.

Narrow dirt roads—often rendered impassable by winter storms and spring mud—presented a challenge to early motorists.

Eight

FACES FROM THE PAST

Three generations of the Sargent family paused from their daily routine to pose on the front steps of their home for an unknown photographer. Perhaps it was late spring. The slats on the closed blinds, or shutters, allowed cooling breezes to flow through the house, while their dark color discouraged bugs from doing the same. The house also served some unknown commercial purpose, as indicated by the sign protruding from behind the left door blind.

Brig. Gen. Thomas Edward Greenfield Ransom was born in Norwich in 1834 and entered Norwich University 14 years later. In the Civil War, he commanded a brigade in the 17th Army Corps and was wounded in four battles. He died of dysentery while on active duty in 1864. "And thus passed away the young, brave, and handsome soldier who when told he only had a few hours to live said, 'I am not afraid to die. I have met death too often to be afraid of it now.' "

These five Loveland siblings—Aaron, Reuben, Ellen, William, and Charles—were born in the 1820s. They were the grandchildren of Joseph Loveland, a Connecticut settler who arrived in Norwich by foot in 1779, carrying a 200-pound bag of grain on his shoulder. Joseph settled on fertile river land a mile and a half north of Norwich village, and his numerous descendants grew up to be farmers, legislators, lawyers, and teachers.

This Civil War portrait of Thomas K.G. Wright, a civil engineer born in Norwich in 1838, was taken shortly after he enlisted in 1861 and was corporal in Company B, 6th Regiment of Vermont Volunteers. His grandfather, John Wright, was one of the town's original settlers from Connecticut.

Cabinetmaker James B. Tracy, who would one day bequeath his property for the erection of a new town hall, was born in Norwich in 1844. At age 18 he volunteered to fight in the Civil War, in Company K of the 16th Vermont Regiment. His nine months of service must have left an indelible mark, as he chose to be photographed in his cavalry uniform some 30 years later.

George Albert Converse was born in 1844 and attended Norwich schools and Norwich University before graduating first in his class from the Naval Academy in 1865. From the rank of ensign in 1866, he went on to become a rear admiral in 1904, commanding the USS *Enterprise*, the cruiser *Montgomery* in the Spanish-American War, and the battleship *Illinois*. He was nationally known as an authority on torpedoes. President Taft attended his funeral at Arlington Cemetery.

Childhood friends May Nye and Emma Slack pose in 1895. May later moved to California. Emma, known for her strong will and sense of humor, married Josiah Huntley in 1903 and lived all her life on her family's farm at the corner of Main and Turnpike. For years, Emma traveled by wagon or sleigh to teach music as far away as Fairlee. One of her many civic achievements was to get the road paved to the Ledyard Bridge, where cars used to "sink out of sight" in the mud.

Leona Willey was one of three daughters of Justin Willey, whose large family moved to Norwich from Sharon after the Civil War. She and her doll dressed their best for this occasion.

Minnie Davis (center) was born in Norwich in 1870 and taught in local schools for several years. This studio photograph, taken about 1910, depicts a teacher and two of her graduating students, Barbara Goss and Anna Hawley, for whom she holds obvious affection. The image recalls a day of linen dresses, hair ribbons, shoe bows, gold pocket watches, and lockets.

Charles and James Huntley grew up in the house at the corner of Main and Turnpike, where their father Josiah, a Nova Scotia native, worked 140 acres of in-town farmland. Their grandfather, the enterprising Charles Slack, had owned the farm at the time of the town's centennial in 1861, when he planted all the trees along Turnpike Road as far as his land extended. Jim Huntley gave the town's playing fields, once part of his family's farm, in memory of his parents.

Photographs of infants in flowing white gowns (such as this 1905 portrait, probably of Ruby Fitzgerald) were popular Victorian expressions of innocence. While infant mortality was much reduced by the turn of the 20th century, photographic studios were often employed to capture the fleeting, fragile months of babyhood. This child is propped up with the assistance of a body brace, which is concealed by the billowing christening gown.

One of the best-known family names in Beaver Meadow continues to be Wallace, represented here by a formal portrait of Eunice and Charles Wallace, a farming couple married in 1895. Eunice was instrumental in raising funds to build the Beaver Meadow Chapel. For years afterward, Eunice organized community dinners and card parties there, while Charles tended the wood stove and cared for the building.

Charlotte Emerson Partridge, 14, poses on the occasion of her 1920 eighth-grade graduation with her grandfather, Capt. William Partridge. Both were descendants of settler Samuel Partridge and his son Alden, founder of Norwich's military academy. William Partridge was himself educated at Norwich University, became a surveyor of railroads and coal mines, and later served in the Civil War. He died five years after this picture was taken, at the age of 97.

Harvey Ladd and Otis Metcalf rest their hands for a formal portrait in 1886. Both operated large farms in Norwich for many years. Otis grew up in Royalton and married Hattie Dutton; they inherited the well-known Dutton Hill farm from her family.

Katie Olds, born in 1865, was one of the six daughters of dry-goods merchant Erastus W. Olds and his second wife, Harriet Ensworth. Katie's half-brother, Edward Olds, ran a general store next to the inn, on the site of today's Dan & Whit's.

Deacon John Dutton, born in 1818, was the third generation to farm his ancestral acres on Dutton Hill. He married Harriet Lord of Union Village in 1849 and had six children, one of whom married Otis Metcalf (opposite page). In addition to raising sheep and horses, the deacon was a devoted member of the Congregational Church and represented Norwich in the state legislature in the 1870s.

Mary Lawrence joined an old and numerous Norwich family when she married Joseph Perkins Hutchinson in 1902. She was a charter member of the Norwich Women's Club and secretary of the Library Association for 40 years.

Susan Boardman (left), who died in 1924 at the age of 99, joins her sister-in-law, Mrs. Walter Scott Hazen (right), with their friend Mary Paul. Mrs. Hazen, the wife of a busy farmer, was a robust soprano in the Congregational Church choir and lived in this house, a former stagecoach stop, at the foot of Dutton Hill.

The first Cook—a name well known in Norwich today—appeared in town seven generations ago, when three brothers and two sisters ran away from a Shaker settlement in Lancaster, Massachusetts. One of the brothers was Samuel Cook, who built this "Home Place" on New Boston Road with his wife, Anna Pratt. They were buried on the homestead in the mid-1800s, and their nine children included Leonard Cook, pictured in the foreground with his wife, Cordelia Roberts.

When Connecticut settler Paul Brigham built the first house on Brigham Hill in 1788, it was the first of several Brigham homesteads there. Two of his descendants were sisters Annie and Grace, who grew up on Brigham Hill.

The original home of Paul Brigham, who served as Vermont lieutenant governor from 1796 to 1813 and from 1815 to 1820, remained in his family for more than a century. In 1890, some of his descendants gathered for an outdoor portrait on Brigham Hill. Seated on the rock are Andrew Brigham and his young son Paul Andrew; behind them at right are his daughters, Annie and Grace, several years older than they appear in the portrait above.

Francis (Frank) Bragg, shown around 1912 with his wife, Cora Fellows Bragg, was the third generation of his family to farm the 150 acres at the top of Bragg Hill Road. In addition to caring for fields and livestock, Frank drove down the hill once a week in his buggy or pung sleigh to sell his butter at Merrill's store; he kept it fresh in between trips by hanging it down the well house. Frank and Cora boarded the teacher from the nearby schoolhouse, although they had no children of their own.

Willey Hill, formerly known as Armstrong Hill, was renamed after the family who moved to Norwich from Sharon in the late 19th century. In 1906 Fred Willey (shown here) bought Fred Hawley's store at the corner of Main Street and Beaver Meadow Road, and it was known as Willey & Smith until 1915. Fred's sister was Minnie Fitzgerald, who owned a millinery shop and helped run the telephone system out of her home on Main Street.

This group of Hutchinsons and Lovelands were all related by blood or marriage to Samuel Hutchinson, who arrived in Norwich in 1765 and cleared a Connecticut River island opposite the Loveland homestead and planted it with corn: "There were not two acres of cleared land in town at that time." The generation shown here includes several great-grandchildren of Samuel, mostly born around 1820.

Mary Davis and Charles Leroy Aldrich were married in 1922. They had a farm on Brigham Hill before buying the large brick "Seven Nations House" on Beaver Meadow Road, which they operated as the Colonial Rest in the 1930s and 1940s. Mary loved birds, devoting an entire room to a gigantic cage for up to three hundred parakeets, finches, and canaries. One of their five children, Maurice, was prominent in business and civic affairs in Hanover and Norwich for many years.

In 1905, chair-factory founder Leslie "Spencer" Patterson posed for a portrait with his granddaughter, Helen Vera Patterson (1903–1961). Helen later attended the Pompanoosuc District School, where she "earned strong A's." Active in Norwich affairs in the 1940s and 1950s, she led an early effort to save the covered bridge in Pompanoosuc. She was also a teacher in Union Village and at Bradford Academy, and later became children's librarian at the Howe Library in Hanover.

Laura and Glen Parker were mainstays in Norwich for many years. Glen ran a meat business from 1921 to 1957, making deliveries by cart to nearby towns and operating a butcher's shop next to his brick house on Main Street. Every May, he drove 25 to 40 head of cattle from his Main Street home to summer pasture out Union Village Road. He was especially proud of his teams of steer and heavy oxen, which he showed for more than 20 years at the Norwich Fair.

Royal Edward Cook and his wife, Louisa, chose a cornfield for the background of this portrait. Royal was born in 1839 on the homestead built by his grandfather, Samuel Cook, and served variously as town lister, selectman, and highway commissioner.

Zenas M. Coleman moved to Norwich in 1868 and lived on Maple Hill Farm just off Union Village Road—first with his parents, then with his sister, and later with his wife, Celia Hurlbutt of Hanover Center, whom he married in 1893. Shown here around 1917, Zenas was a prominent deacon in the Congregational Church, and Celia was president of the Norwich Woman's Missionary Society. Their daughter Louise continued to run the farm with her husband, Albert Johnson, until 1968.